Doors to Ancient Poetical Echoes

"Journeys through the Door"

By George E.

iUniverse, Inc.
Bloomington

Doors to Ancient Poetical Echoes
Journeys through the Door

iUniverse books may be ordered through booksellers or by contacting:

iUniverse
1663 Liberty Drive
Bloomington, IN 47403
www.iuniverse.com
1-800-Authors (1-800-288-4677)

ISBN: 978-1-4620-3552-6 (sc)
ISBN: 978-1-4620-3553-3 (e)
ISBN: 978-1-4620-3554-0 (dj)

Printed in the United States of America

iUniverse rev. date: 8/9/2011

Table of Contents

Dedication

Dedicated to Supreme family and the Ancestors, my family, love and
Light
Give Thanks
GES

Introduction

Is it time to hear the echoes we hear and can and can't identify. Whispers are in our mind and heart of which we are a part,. 'Doors to Ancient Poetical Echoes' expresses these thoughts, words and rhymes in kind. These words can be enlightening or healing. Think strong and speak up, then think healing thoughts even when thinking of others. Do you remember your ancestors?

Do you like going beyond yourself, your mind, then read on. It is enticing and provocative in its own way. It will tantalize you into traveling at light speed and take you beyond this earth. Happy voyage and enjoy. This is all for your entertainment. Be happy you read this and share it with your best friends along with my other books

The poem 'Ancient Echoes" will start you in the right direction and put you on the glide path. Enjoy this thought provoking dialogue dedicated to taking you to another environment where you can become the astronaut, so take off and happy landing! Here is an excerpt:

Ancient Echoes

Left right
Way to go
Now can do
All asked
Because
You are ancient
Love the old
Heart is whole
Ancient echoes
Ring below

And above
The echo
Of your song.......
Mind singing
All on hold
Now many
Now unfold
So you can see
Ancients
Around you
Want you to be
Immortal!

Ancient the Sound

Ancient the sound
Homeward bound
On the way
To you being you
Each and every day
Young can't do it
Mature as you are
Doesn't make you there
But living and loving and teaching
Young and old
Makes you almost ancient
To the folks you know
Echoes ring in your ear
Like rings in a tree
You are encumbered
Not yet free
For the ancients
Can see clearly what is now
And what is it to be
Why give advice
To all those in need
So you can show
You are the Ancients indeed!

Creating History

Life
Love
History
Pages of thought
Lives living
People making
Through the ages
Wondering, why they have
Is it to create history?
I don't know
Do you?
Wishing for the story
Waiting for the theme
Acting like there is a punch line
On your life
Why history, says as history does
But why do you follow along,
History
Takes you on this trip
Many trips
Until you realize
You are tripping
Through history
Toe tipping
Smart living
Just so you can say
You are making history!

Doors

Doors different doors
Doors open
Doors close
Doors lock
Doors unlock
Doors single
Doors double
Doors on the left
Doors on the right
Doors straight ahead
Doors behind
Which door do you find
For you
Doors real
Doors of the mind
Is yours open
Or closed
New or old
Is it cold
Or warm
Is it there
Or is it gone
Is the door of your heart waiting
Or are you sitting in the dark
Instead of dating
Thinking you put it in the bank
And are saving it
For no one else but you
Or are you not opening the door
Unless they are due

Doors are meant to open

Not to be nailed shut
While you sit in a rut
Thinking it is best shut
Not realizing you can't go out
Or invite other hearts in
Including all of your kin
You think you know it all
Open the doors of your mind
And you will know much more
Open Divines' door
And find out what you are here for
The right relationship is behind
One of those doors
Thinking it is and was wrong
So open the door where
The light shines bright
And know that opening certain doors is right
And success is in sight!

I Answer My Door

The door bell rings
I hear it in the distance
I wonder who fate brings to my door
I listen intensely
As the sound of the bell
Rings and echoes in my ear
A familiar sound,
I have heard throughout the ages
Making me pay attention
To you and me
Bringing back that sound
That lets me know
I have what I have been looking for.
Surreal as I open the door
Only to see
No one is there
Maybe I missed them
Since I took too long
To hear you calling me
Getting my attention
That I am here
And you are there
Waiting for my answer,
I respond
As the memory appears of you
When I heard the bell before
And you suddenly appeared
Expecting not expecting you at my door
Next time I will run
And open so you can
See me straight up
Without all the fanfare!

Life In An Instant

Life in an instant
Playing that song
Violins leaping
Playing our song
I have been waiting
To **live** all life long
And win life in an instant
Is all forlorn
I breathe life
In an instant
And know no need
To wait to live
Be and realize
Life is in every instance
So **live** life now
And long!

Incessant Living

Life stalks life
Life is old
New and bold
Souls are leaving
To let you know
That you are reaping
All is about to unfold
So live and be You, Soul
And know we are with you
Through this and more
Until you soar
On to God's glory
Beyond this shore!

Is It Yours, Is it Mine

Is it your life
Is it mine
Is it your life
Is it my life
Why am I here
Why you come?
To see me
To see you
To meet We
Are you my sister
Are you my brother
Are you my mother
Am I your sister
Am I your Father
Am I your blood brother
Are you here for me
Am I here for you
Don't you know
Can't you see
Is it you
Or is it me
Am I asleep
Or is this a dream
Did you know me before
Are you here to continue
Or to close the door
Are you following me
Or am I on your trail
Searching for my loved one
Who was gone
But now has come
To find my long lost relative

My love betrothed to me
By time immortal
Transforming time
Reaching beyond galaxies
So we can be together
Especially when we said forever
But I don't recognize you or me
It is you
Or is it me
Because you don't seem to recognize me either
And you act like we never met
Or like I owe you a debt
And it is time to pay
And the time to collect is this day
Which keeps me asking?
Is it you
Or is it me
Or is it yours or is it mine?

Your Eye See Your Eye Want

Hungry
Eat
Can't see
Wait look up
Jah here to help you
Why you can't see me,
For looking
I want much
It is not to be
If you can't see
You want all
You want what they got
Yourself
On your own
Enough is what you need
Can't have it all
But can have what you want
Just don't hurt anyone else
And take theirs
For we are all here to share
But my eyes want what my eye see
Like the birds and the bees
I can try and fly high
Grab what I can
But it is too much
For you to handle
See what is for you
And not what is for me
See what is for you
Don't take what is for me
Don't be selfish
Share what you have

With whom you love
Don't be greed
Because your eye want
What your eye see
Blesses are me
Who can see.......Others
And making sure what
We need we get
Not what we want
Because it may be too much
For us to handle
And we won't learn
You can't have what
Your eyes see, your eyes want
And we will learn to
Take only what we can eat
Digest from the feast
We have before us
And not let greed
Push us beyond our brink
And cause us to sink
And just take for taking sake
Because we want
What our eye can see!

What Passes Under a Bridge

Water passes under a bridge
The bridge I see
And from where I am I can see the water
How high it is and how low it goes
The bridge is a path to the other side
There she waits
I wait looking at her
Her past goes by
I care and care not
Just like the water that passes by
I watch to see if I recognize
Her life
I watch and wonder where the water goes
I wonder why it is always,
Hurrying on its way
To where?
Who is waiting?
Who is watching?
To see if they can see.

My, the water looks the same
As it did yesterday
As I contemplate the sky
Looking on guard
I watch this water pass on by
Why does it just look
When does it see the water rise up
To meet it
Shake hands
Trade stories
Of life on earth and all in its path
Or is it silent until it hears the lightning

Then I look again
To see if I recognize my water
Does it belong to me
Is it mixed in with the other waters
Or is it separate
Powerful
Surging onto its destiny
Helping the fish to swim home
And boats to arrive at their port
And then return in full cycle
Successful
Tipping its hat as it passes
Under the bridge once again
On its way to where?
I don't know but I see her on the
Other side looking too
Into the water wondering if
My water is with her water
She looks and nods hoping I understand
Or know
If our water is now traveling together
And will it pass this way again
Will we recognize it?
And know we are together
Or will we ignore it as many do
On their way to where ever
Separated by this bridge
Not realizing a bridge may separate
But water travels together
Even if we don't recognize it when
It comes pass this bridge again!

Water

Rushing water
Bringing all to you
Then leaving as
Swift as it came
You thought it was
Like your relationship
Not understanding
That either they are blowing in the wind
Or flowing like water
Smooth or rough
Choppy or wavy.
Crying makes a lot of noise
But quiet is the lake
Before the ocean
Of the storm
Tsunami in the making
Like a pissed off woman
Trying to get your claim to fame
You see the water but don't know
If it is long enough
To recognize it as yours
Temporary is the flow
Even after you drink it
Going through channels
Only to converse
And seek its' own level
Not controlled by anyone
Including you.
Water so soothing
You forget it destroys
Anything in its path
When it is in full flight and moving

Flooding you and your minds
With thoughts
Bloated with or without fish
Searching for a breath
And then raging before it takes its rest
Water, peaceful and yet so powerful
It is more than a handful
For you to hold
Like two women following
You on a trip down river
On a raft rocking to and fro
Making you not sure if you
Want to come or go
You will know water
A wave or a drip
That can tear up your house
Or take you on an unbelievable trip
Water is good for you…
Or tell Katrina folks that tip!

Ancient Waters

Ancient waters
Come and go
Up and down
From the sky to the ground
Hilltops flow
That is the way the water goes
Ancient waters
That we sow
Reap the whirlwind
They say
Bottled water
Why today
Where is my ancient water
That is now gone
And new water is here to stay
Water before
Chemicals today
Who took my ancient water
Same criminal with a private waterway
Ancients drunk out of the lake
Where do we drink when the water is all taken
Bottled, strained and baked
And sold to us
Is the mistake
Now we are scared to drink
From the tap
Now water has a bad rap
If not bottled
But we don't know what is under the cap
I want my ancient water back
You keep your leeching plastic
You now understand better

That is on the store stacked rack
Ancient waters feed the fish
That ends up on our dish
We not understanding
What the fish drink
But they are suffering from thirst
Drugged up fish are
Ending up having problems
Trying to navigate
Their way home
And end up on shore
Asking for a glass
Of clean water
But please not from the store
Ancient water brings history
Some new water brings misery
Controlled by who
Is a privatized mystery
Since most today have
No wisdom
They are doing all kinds of
Things that are risky
We better keep our eye
On our water and not on the gas
Because the new bottle is wearing a mask
And the real water is being siphoned
And before you know it, the end
Product will only be a rash
So when you drink even from the
Tap or the bottle
Ask what's in it
Is it ancient water?
Ahh tastes good,
Good for you
Or is it the new bottled plastic and
now it is called mountain dew?

The Echoes of Shame

Echoes of shame
Echoes of game
Echoes of the same
Sounding but loud
Crescendos abound
Ringing thru time immemorial
Making waves that
Let us know this is the same game
No change
Why do we play?
Basketball is a sport
Wars have been fought
For what
The game don't change
Noise is loud
Music is melody
I harmonize in my mind
When I hear a song
Singing inside
Speechless sometime
Don't mean I am a mime
Even though others seem to act out
Lame one act plays
Of the same old shame
Shameless game
Trying to tell me it is all the same
Then, now and in the future
Reverberating don't claim to
Be the beginning of the echo
Or the end of the sounds
We claim it started from
Or the mess we lay blame

Only to mimic it and say it is ours
Because we take it over
And claim we invented it
Even though the Ancients
Had the same
Echoes as their claim to fame
Stolen later
Sold as an original
When no one is here to claim…
It is just an echo from
Ancient days
When the original sound was created
And now we have an echo of the same!

Here After

Who is here
After
I am gone
You
Me
We
Them
They
No way
I am here now
Why wait
To see me
I see you now
Why wait
Time moves on
Where did the time go?
You were wasting
As it passed you by
They told you to wait
Why?
Slow
Speed kills,
They say
Move faster
Slow gives
You time
To miss this bus
And then you have
To wait
For the next
I am here now
Won't wait

For you to move
Forward
If you can't see
It is fine
No waiting
Procrastination is an event
Not worth waiting for
Find the time
To make up your mind
So get a move on
And then
I can meet you
Or I will not be here
I came to see you
I will go
You will come
Only after
I am gone!

Fill Up

You so young
You so old
It is time to fill up
and behold
That an empty cup
Can carry a lot
A full cup can not
Sponges soak up until they are full
People hope they can carry their own
Full or empty
They wish for more
Fill up
Not the food on the table
But the food that feeds the Soul
And helps you control
Your emotions
Open your intellect
Turn on wisdoms faucet
Turn off and release that anger
That weighs you down
Fill up on happiness
For it is filled with wealth
And it will make you laugh
 And believe you are stealth
Able to handle anything
That is before you
And then you can dump the not necessary
And take up the destiny
Which is primary,
Once the secondary is dumped
And now you have room in your cup
To fill it up
To the brim with love
Instead of beer and rum!

Past Tense

Past tense
Present tense
Old tense
New tense
Which are you
I dream of whom
Jeanie with the light brown hair
Why, where
That is the past
Jeanie is not here
Sue, I don't know where
The presence is now
Future coming soon
At a theater near you
Home is for the heroes
In the past
Presently there are the unsung
Singing their songs
Why wait to hear
Make your own song
Right or wrong
Just sing
Now and forever
So you can feel
You belong
Past due
Present fun
Future more sun
Wipe the tears away
And let the past go
To the place it came from
For the making of the future
Is before you in the present
And the past has passed on!

Ancient

Ancient
Is my mind
Spirit here and now
Waiting to heal all
Ready or not
Breathe
And feel me why
You can't hear me now
Sounds abound
Reverb into the Round
Traveling at light speed
Into your heart
Cleaning away the knots
Not for you to ignore
What you came for
The Ancients are here
What are you waiting for,
My dear
Ring the bell
Sound the trumpets
For the time is upon you
Waiting for you
To listen
Believe
See
Retrieve
And know it is time to receive
And thank the Ancients
And live in peace!

Old Chinese Saying

They say women hold up half the sky
Why
Who holds up the other half?
Do they stand by themselves?
Are they alone?
Or are they love
Where is the mime
The person playing to them
Pretending they are not a part of them
Where is the man
Who is the sky?
Why is the world spinning
To the tune of women willing
To hold up half the sky
Why?
Man must help them
Now I understand why they sigh
And want to cry
Men must do their part
And hold up the other half of the sky
Or are we just to shine
And sparkle in the sunlight
Like a ray
And have another do the job
That has been ordained to us
That is a must
That creates a lot of fuss
Because if it is not done
What we know as mankind can turn to dust
Or is it that mothers make babies
To help them hold up the sky
While men are out doing

Hard as they try
To support the Sun
And shine
Or is it the Divine
That bears a ray
Of Light upon the earth
To wake the men
To get up and be a ray
With one hand
And hold the sky with the other
As Earth rests on their head
As it spins, around.

Five Element Thinking

Five element thinking
I am fire
She is water
Together water can put out fire
Or we can get together and
Create steam
How hot is that
I am earth
She is water
Water covers the earth
But will soften my hard exterior
And penetrate into my interior
As I relax and accept her to settle peacefully
I am water
She is earth
She tries to cover me but I cover her
As I can spread myself thin
And seep into her valley filling it up
As I run down her mountain
I create a free fall upon her
Striking her playfully to bounce
along her way
She is wood
I am metal, We meet and greet
I came from her and I am glad
To see my mother as she celebrates
my strength
I am metal, she is fire
She fires me up all the time which
Causes me to be shaped by her design
And I am able to change myself
Since now with her I am more flexible

And can change from my previously cold,
Stiff demeanor I displayed before
With her heat she melts me
As I feel her all over
I am wood she is earth
I grow from her and she nourishes me
So I can grow so tall, so full
I am celestial as I reach the sky
I am the majestic tree born
From my mother who is proud of me
Because I gave birth to air
Oxygen for all the people to breathe
All the plants applaud my mother
And we all show off every day in the sun
As air approaches we realize
That we can breathe in all that matters
And we can show how the whole family
Works together
We are the five elements thinking that
You need us, we are family
We think alike
We support each other
We help each other to grow especially fire
 Because air has helped fire grow so big
As water helps to push up through the universe
At the same time as water quenches our thirst and
Helps wood grow along with our food
As metal steps in and helps us build our house
And a great fire
So as we walk the earth with Mother
We appreciate our family
We are thinking we are in balance and the best!

Do Yoga

Stretch you mind
Gluts scream for help
Tight is the chest
Mind not open
Pull, push, and pry it apart
Mind is strong
Weak is the breath
Breathe in
Breathe out
Don't doubt
Just do Yoga
So you can change
Open fold
Flex that ability
Comes when you do Yoga
Small steps long is the life
Long is the limb
Smiling is not a whim
Flex the mind
The soul is bold
And can go further
Then you can go
Stretch and rest
Relax and know
You are young, old
Connected to the Divine
Yoga of the Soul
Laugh or pray
Is the way
To go beyond the movements
So you can see the goal
Ancient Yoga
For the young and the old
Do Yoga!

Rest

Rest
Let life unfold
From the beginning
To the end
And to the beginning
Let it open
Like a rose
Shining brightly
New like stories untold
Rest
Trust more
Not less
See the good
Not any mess
Live the life
Without too much strife
Rest
Play the song
Be strong
Don't do wrong
For life is the good
For you to be
So others can see
That it is not all bad
That people not need to be sad
Stress is a lack of rest
Seeing life as the best
So rest
Don't fret
Don't waver
Life like good food
You must savor

For the sweet is to the sweet
And life's' love is for you to keep
And share
With those who you care
And want you to preserve
Even when it is a lot to bear
Rest
Let go of the tension
Learn the lesson
To be well and rested!!

Sleep

Rest
Sleep
Weep
No strain
Rain
Sun shines
On me
Life
Best
Trip
Rest
Trouble
Game
Stress
Fun
Drink less
Do rest
Be at sleep
When it is time
So you can see
The day time chime
Noise
Quiet
Peace
Love
Wake or sleep
Peace need to be
Inside
Outside
All it means
To be awake
Or to sleep

At night
So days can be full
Of life
And more
Breathe
In between
Smile
Don't be mean
Tired
Awake
Restful sleep
A bed to make
Fat is the mattress
For sleeping is the best
Are you awake
Or sleep
Now or later
Open your eyes
When asleep
Close your eyes
When you are awake
Know it is called
The dream way
Awake
Then open your eyes
Close when asleep
Until you hear the alarm clock beep!

Where is the Place We Live

Where is the place we live?
Where do we go?
Where to be
Where to know
Why is life sow
Learn the way
Each and every day
Then the Tao
Will see you
Play each day
In your own way
Bless the time
We spend
Worry not about
What
Which way
And how come no say
Talk and know
When it is quiet
So you can listen
To words
That inspire
You to be where you are going
Arrive where you are to be
Need to get there early
Don't be late
Because today is the day
Where you are
Where you go
Where you need to be
Now this day
Or tomorrow!

Seize the Day

Seize the day
Grab for it
Strive to be it
For today is almost gone
Tomorrow will come
Quietly
Then leap upon you in the morn
And burst upon the plate
As if a grand meal
Savor it
Lick it eat it up
For looking at it will
Only make it spoil
Fresh is the dew
Before it melts
The snow is fresh
Before the fall
Water is crisp in the lake
But still in the battle
As it sits and waits
For a drink
Now is the time to
Seize the day
Before it gets away
From you
Or someone tries to steal it away
Solve the mystery of now
Later won't wait
Forever is not due
You are waiting too long
Seize it
Grab it

Run
Chase
But be there first
So you can see it come
And take the advantage
To make it
Delay tomorrow
Because you have taken up so much
Of it
It takes time to collect
Itself
And realizes it owes you
Not you owe it
Or miss that payment
To be broke
Out of health
Out of wealth
And waiting on another day
For a hand out
Only to say
You missed it
And didn't get paid
Don't wait
Do what you planned
Put off
Thought about
Procrastinated
And then
Seize the day
Make it pay!
Wealth comes in the day
In the night
In every way
Money is money
Wealth is health
Mind is Soul
Soul is gold
Spirit is everlasting!

Escape

Escape up or escape down
Or free or trapped
Is everything put in your lap
Is their rich or poor
Is their windows or doors
That we see and go through
Do we escape
Or are we trapped
Are we trying to get free
Or is it we just want to,
Be left to just be
Is it necessary to choose
Or is there such a thing as win or lose
Is this the way to fall into the trap
Or just jump into it
From the traps of society
Or are we as free
But scared it will hug you back
Because it realizes what you have
And what you lack
Trees are free to grow
But maybe they feel trapped
But trees see you can be free
Because you can move and be
And just not sway in the breeze
But you're afraid sometimes to take necessary steps
To do what is in your best interest
For your own sake
Because like the gazelle runs free
When it is about to be trapped
The trapped bird will fly free
When its cage is opened inadvertently

So should we if we,
Feel we are not being the best we can be
And if you don't understand
Fly to new heights
So you can see what I see..........!

Justice Wears a Blindfold

Justice is blind only so it can't see
or be a witness to the past, present and future injustices
that is to be
where truth runs like a horse fleeing from a group of marauding fleas
and crimes that are committed in the name of justice.
The statue in the court house should be changed to the three monkeys
don't see, don't speak, and don't hear
and then we can add a fourth monkey
one that doesn't care!

Free

Are we not born free?
Can't we freely see?
All that is before us
Isn't it true the birds sing
Because they are free
Free to fly high or low
Reaping from their journey
What they sow
Can't they fly – fly higher
Can the mountain goat climb or leap
Can't the student try to reap
What they enthrall
The lion roams free
The elephant is all he can be
In the jungle
Why do monkeys swing
Or climb a tree
And the moon back
In the sun lights glaze
Like a shoe shine in the day
Breath is free
We breathe as we can
But smoke imbues our breath
And the sea although free
Doesn't give a damn
Just moves and waves to be free
Flowing to and fro
Free to seek its' own level
While man tries to
Stagnate other men's growth
Block families from knowing
That they are free

To be
All they can be
Babies free to cry
Women dream of freedom
While they sigh
Because their babies
Fight for someone else's lie
And (we) should be able
To set you free
At least from the liar
Who needs to believe
He is who he says he is
But makes you believe
You can go where you please
As long as you obey
What society deems
For its oppressors
As they take advantage
To float, to boat
And trample on other people's dreams
Free is the bee
Who uses his stinger
And freely pollinates flowers
For you and me
The sun shines freely
As we speak
Of rainy days
As animals hide from becoming lunch
And politicians from congress flee
Before making good decisions
They never complete
So does the tree
Feel the ability to be free
But realizes it must stand
For something
Instead of relinquishing its throne
Like royalty
Can you truly be free
If your mind is not

And you can't get your ass to follow
Or do you not listen
To the willow in the wind
The song in the breeze
When you quiet the tendency
Try and block others
Who are trying to be free
Free yourself and others will follow
Free to walk your path
And flow the way
The light of the ray
For love is really free!

Old Stories, New Stories

Life, old, new
Stories they tell
What you want to hear
Old new
Versus
New old
Future talk, new
But they still tell the old
The new want to hear the old
The old want to hear the new
What is your song
I can tell
Those who know you well
My life story
Is telling you to
Be your own story
Make it new then old
Then new
Like the future foretold
So I can believe
Your stories
New or old
You like your role
And then I will tell you
My stories about life
And the Soul.

Travel the Dusty Trail

Travel the dusty trail
Where does it lead
See the corn grow
Roll over the husk
Flies retreat to unknown residences
Awaiting the next delivery
Of fertilizer
Wheat grows day and night
As birds sleep in flight
Only to be swept upward
By the wind
As the sun comes across the horizon
All bows and awakes
To this quiet symphony
Playing each and every song
Worth listening
Until it warms your very gut
Strings like a harp
Awaiting its master
Snow capped mountains stand majestically
Upon the plain
Back dropped by the blue sky
Like painters who have completed
Their master pieces
As sailors go to sea to
Feel the power of the waves
To know they are alive
Playing amongst the fish
Who dive to prove...
Their swimming is an art
Done by pros singing
How low can you go?

The strum of the lutist
Sounds a very good tune
That travels out to
Reach a distant ear
As those close hear nothing
But the twang of the strings
As a whistler whistles a tune
Too plain to reveal
His souls' flight to thee
Wishing love would grace
His window sill
As birds leap for joy
And try to copy this theme
Steps in the soil
Reveal they had been here before
But where do they lead
Where did they go?
Only the sparrow knows
What the owl has told
For night covers the tracks
And the dew covers the trail
So brave warriors can't follow
But have to carve their own way
To the top
So they can say
They did it their way
And the frog leaps over
The children while playing their games
Not knowing one day they will
Travel this way
Not on the same path
But paths will cross if only for a day
As lakes and rivers map which way
To follow
So their boat won't drift
Without delay
And arrive at the correct port
Before loved ones go away tomorrow!!

Chasing a Dream

Chasing a dream
Where does it go
Does it hide
Does it elude for a better dream outcome
Does it make a grand entrance
Or does it appear like a cloud of dust
To be blown away by a strong wind
Dreams come and go
To where
How high
How far
Does it hide its face?
Or smiles upon your breastplate
Looking for a way in
Or is it like a surfer
Riding the high wave
Into your heart
A dream, does a dream become a light,
A reality, a nightmare
That it will go and never return
Or do dreams appear when you awake
And you think you are asleep
Can you see the beginning
Or the end?
Results, does a dream make
For whose sake
Partial or final
Can you remember?
What was said?
The outcome
Is it meant to be?
Or is it not reality

Does it tickle your fancy or imagination?
Or play upon the mind
As unfulfilled wishes
Needs, wants
Pleadings for you to follow
Entertain, make happen
Or does the dream display
A picture, landscape
A Video of what could be
If only you would wake up
And realize dreams do come true!

The Traveler

The traveler goes
And comes
And goes again
Where I don't know
He goes
She's there
He comes
And goes again
Where she does not know
Traveling
Going to places known
Unknown
To who knows
Where he goes.
It's places
New, young and some so old
Ancient places
Visited by the bold
Out of the way
Isolated
Made ready for him to come
Then go
Is this traveling or
Going to come
Back to visit
Since she is there waiting
For him to show
So many places to go
See be
And wonder
How many more places to see
He cares

And cares not
For he has seen so many places
Wherever he goes
He feels at home
Met many people
So many faces
Some warm some cold
Some young some old.
Ancient places
High is the moon
He travels far beyond
The universe is his
As he travels to the sun
Long is the time
But to the traveler
Time is here
And gone
So is he
As he comes then is gone
She waits for him to come
Then she will go
This time with him
When the traveler comes
Encumbered no more
She will be free
To go then come
With the traveler
When he comes!

Ripple Effect

Ripple effect
Waves
Ripple upon my mind
Soul waves beckon me higher
Flight takes me to new places
As I feel the past
Flying into its own place
And the ripple of my mind
Brings me forward to the present
The ripple of the past
Of giants doing good
Enduring much as
They present forth the Light
Of Wisdom
In order to impart to
Those who are too young
To remember
Their Soul's flight
And their place amongst the heights
I hear the reverberation
Of the present pushing me….
Forward
Not stuck on the past
Letting go of all that kept
Me from the future
As the twang of their letting go
Or their connections releasing them
So they can go anywhere
They need to go
And the ripple effect
Pushing me to where I need to be
I hurry because

The tide comes in
With new hope and inspiration
Dreams made real
Work gets done
And the ripple reveals
The suns light waves
Shining and showing the way
The boat comes to shore
Safe and sound
And all is ok
Because the flow
Round and round
Is the result of the
Ripple of continuity
From then to now
And all can feel the effects
Of the ancestors love flowing
To insure we are
Living up to our expectation
On our throne wearing our crown!!!!

The Dance of Life

Wonder what's going on
Before and after
You think you know
It is called the dance of life
Wanna dance
Can you
Get jiggy with it
Can you see
The forest from the trees
The bees from the stinger
The mean from the derivation
Or are you blind
Can't see
Can't hear
The sound from the falling
Of the trees in the forest
Open up your ears
Eyes can see
Unless you are too blind
To see
What is in front of your feet
Step on dodo
Why
Dogs shit their way thru life
Do you too
Can you not smell the odor
The funk from your own
Beeswax
Or are you mad
You've been mistreated
The dance of life
Are we doing the dance?

Or are we watching the
Dancers dance
And we are a witness to the first
Party to the second
Testifying
To what we see and observe
And can't believe our eyes or ears
Or what we hear
Or what they are saying
What are we saying?
Are we clear
Succinct able to
Articulate our position
Or are we just doing
A two step
To their waltz
And think we can cha cha
Our way out of it
Or is this too much
To believe
What has transpired
Is actually real
Did it happen
Is it all a dream
Or are we dancing
Soca style
To a reggae beat
That spits lyrics so deep
We can't understand
What we hear
Or what we see
So discombobulated
We think we are not seeing
Not hearing what we are hearing
We are not a party to
Not witnessing this
In real time
Real life
And the bullshit stacked on the walls

Is not real, it will just fall
When we open up
Stop the jive step
Just for a little while
While they grind their way
To a slow beat
Of your brain
Fried on drugs
Or brain washed and scrambled
Until toast
Any way you slice it
You are washed up
And break dancing won't
Save your ass
So it can follow
You away from all of this
Nonsense made real
By notes surreal
You tango to a salsa beat
Eat poisoned or raw meat
And call yourself human
Now that's a feat
Dance, dance, dance
To life's melodic beat
Until you dervish into a trance
And ask where is the
Song for the last dance
But the beat goes on
More stuff more muss
For us to fuss
About is shown
And we turn on the TV which is a plus
For we can see the stuff
We argue about
And wonder who is watching us
While we are watching them
Two way ignorance, is a must
So we can't see what is before us
Video TV the next generation

In brain washing stunts
Politics as unusual
Followed by 24/7 lust
Shame
And you can win money
Is my game
While the chickens are
Being stolen, tryst and eaten
Children raped and beaten
By those who want us
To trust
And lives are stolen
Peddled, sold, belittled
Without as much as a fuss
From the authorities
Who are busy stuffing their
Turkeys with ten day old bread crust
Convinced that this is all an illusion
Being played in front of us
Like the radio broadcast
Of the war of the worlds
And we thought it was
Just a fake cast
Not a future play
Acted out after 1984
Only to find out it was
A glimpse to the real drama
Unfolding and showing us
That TV made real
Is only a newscast
A front page story
Of who won the best
Dance category
The banks versus the stock brokers
Main Street versus the military
Politicians or typhoid Mary
Predators versus little red riding hood
The democrats versus the republican tea party
Not sure who finished first

Or who finished last because ballet to rock
Was first and it all ended in a twist
With jive first, electric slide
And pole dancing in the advanced categories
Followed up by the winners
Who were given new home contracts
With flexible winning interest rates
And hookers as their take home dates
Oh you watching court on TV
Justice nowhere else for you and me
Still dancing beats a talk
Singing beats a walk
More talk less walk
Is what got us here
And we continue
To two step our way
Thru this mire
And the dance of fire
To witness the dance
The strife, the music
Have gun will travel
Society as we know it unraveled
Not speaking to each other
While we party
To the ass shakin_ vibes
Called the dance of life!

Lessons of the Tree

We grow and grow
Ages pass
By way of the sun
We continue to grow
Water our hopes and dreams
And watch as we blossom
And become, to be
Who we are to be
And we continue
Even though many come and go
In and out of our lives
We watch
Earnestly wondering where
They are going
Do we need to know, or see
Or just watch them grow up
As if a tree
Then watch as they progress
Blossoms multiply
And continue to divide….
And divide
Until they are small as the
Smallest tree, then tall
And become like the forest
Only to continue the cycle
Over and over
While we watch
We circle the world
And see it again and again
Until our rings
And the family of branches
Reach and touch the sky

Connecting in silence
With other trees
In other places
Close and far
Missing those now gone, cut short
Or used to house all the people we see,
Come and go
Around and around
Watching the circle of life
Go full circle
Some learning their lessons, some not
And we say to each other
When will they learn
As we continue to assist them
In ways they know not
Taking us for granted
Like other species
On the planet
But silently we wait until
They see our majestic boughs
As we sway in the wind
Bending to the will of the wind
And loving the warmth of the sun
Enjoying the brotherhood
Of all of us around the world
We soak up with the water
We quench our thirst
For knowledge and
Display our wisdom
Before all in plain view
But many only see
The bark and not the inner tree
Who is meaning, to teach us how to be
So we too can live
Throughout the ages
Multiple rings
Many wisdoms
Many trees!!

So What Does the Forest Say

So what does the forest say
Sitting there quietly
Or so we think
Knowing all of this is going on
Hither and thither
To and fro
What is the problem
What is it they know
We seem to not know
Or recognize
The deep rings show age
But also shows who is the sage
Seen all done all
Of that and more who has passed their way
Who has come and who has gone away
Indifference or is it different
I would say
Do branches grow to remind you
Of your family or ancestral way
Trees are strong
Tree roots grow together
And are very long
Probably from one root
Then now and have gone
On to better things
Forming more groups
But wise to what we do to us
They keep together hoping
We don't come to force them to separate
They do their endless duty
Breathe in the stale air
Out with the fresh

Never take time to rest helping us to breathe and live
They give and receive
How wise they are
They show us because they
Don't cut us down
To the ground
Does a tree fall in the forest
And make a sound
No they quietly watch us
Destroy each other and pollute
The very ground
They live upon!

Don't Argue with Ignorant People

Don't
Don't argue
Don't argue with ignorant
People
What are you going to get
Something intelligent?
Wise?
Mind blowing?
Or dull senseless ramble
Nowhere to go with it
Pulling out you own hair
Stress you can't bear
Frustrated at what you hear
Don't worry
Change comes
Slowly when you try
To change those who are not clear
That ignorance is a cross you don't want to bear
Say less do more
Is what you cannot get
From ignorance
Like a bull stuck on stare
Rearing to go
But no place to see clear
And they only respond
To the color red
Ignorant to the kaleidoscope of other colors
Stuck like a deer
So don't argue with an ignorant person
Just share your knowledge
And hope they understand
A mind is a terrible thing to waste
So use that
Head (or not) called a hat!

Do You Hear the Call

Do you hear
The call
Calling you
Ancient echoes
Bellowing through
With love
And life
So old
Yet so bold
You are who you are
Why ignore
This is what you came for
All is with you
Here now and then
Rebounding from heaven
Answer
Know it is for you
This is your time
Your role
You are who you are
Then and now
Ancient
Young but old
The sounds you hear
Are not from here
But from that voice within
Saying you are who you are
Don't wait
Wake up now
You didn't just come to be
But you can be now
Like the tree

There are many rings
Many times
Round and round
Till you have found
And heard
The ancient echo
Within
Calling you to wake up
And hear
Love's keynote
Chimes
Calling you home
To now be all you can be
Ancient sounds
Echoes saying
You are who you are
I am me
And time for you to be
Who you are supposed to be!

Willow Tree

Willow tree
Blowing in the wind
Green and growing
Relaxing on a nice sunny day
The willow stays
Out of trouble
As it listens to the people, talking
The wind roaring
As it plays along
In its own way
The secret the Willow knows
Is how to flow
And bend, not break
As it lays out in the open
For all to see
Unlike the pine tree
It has listened
To how the bamboo be
It hears, bend not break
Agree, don't agree
And when you hear the roar
Of the wind
Smile, relax and practice
Your flow within
The willow is an example
For all to see
How to go thru life
And how to be
Tall, strong but soft
Stand up, but flow within!

Don't Belong Here

As I look at a tree
I wonder what it has to do with me
Such a wonderful thing to see
The tree you say
I say also people too
Is important to convey
We belong together
The inner and the outer
The omega and the alpha
Oxygen and carbon dioxide
Serve each other
From time immemorial
Breath I say
Both of us breathe
So that we may
Live another day
What is it that made it that way
I wonder do you?
We continue to live
The same as a tree
Long lives and yearn to be free
Branches spread out
As families move apart
Still connected
But separated
Linked together
Rooted by light
Shining from above
We both share water from above
So we can grow
Be tall and more
Learn and shown

All that came and gone
Only to come again
Stronger
Spreading its wings
As wind blows through
To create a song and sing
Whistle a melody
Trees also give energy
To make sure we
Live and can be
And we should give back
So the tree can get what it needs
And stop killing our brother trees
And be like them and how they trust us
And let them be!

Up Down All Around

Up down all around
Is it rain
Or is it pours
Did it rain
Or am I wet
From sweat
Did I cry
Or did I sigh
Did I holler
For a dollar
It is up and down
It is all around
Dust and dirt
Fighting, it ain't worth
Life is up and down
And all around
For some upside down
And all around
They don't understand
It is not part of the plan
But you must keep
The hour glass up
The temperature gauge on top
And then let the cream rise
May you know it
That it is not straight
But round
Yes what comes
Goes around
Did it rain
Or did the sun shine
Don't complain

Rain or shine
We can do all
We came to do it this time
So don't waste it on crime
Or arguing about time is needed
But can't buy health
Health is vital but can't buy wealth
Happiness should be a heartbeat
So we don't have to hear them complain
Because the moon won't wave
And virgins can remain the same
Until they are ready to get married
And become someone's main dame
While spinsters focus on the past
And cry more than it rains
Rain grows things that are great
And babies drink water and eat the food
To become role models if they can
Accomplish their goals or fail
As things go up and down
And all around
So that what you start you can complete
Doesn't change
All the same
As it goes up and down
And round and round!

Past is the Past

Past is the past
Past is present
Present is past
Some say
It is not my way
The past is gone
The present is here today
It is time you realize
It is here
And it has begun
Time stands still for no one
The sun moves on
And waits for no one
Many think they can relive the past
But the past is gone
Chasing a dream
Is like eating ice cream
When you are asleep
Even though you see yourself
The taste escapes you
Thinking you can relive the past
Will prove that it is something you can't do
But the past has lived you
You have out-lived the past
It is like a dream not made to last
But only remind you of the present
Which is sent to you
To let you know
That it is behind you
You must turn around
So the way forward
Is in front of you

Look see
Watch the water past
The fire then the ash
See the sea gulls dash
For a new nest, new heights
As they try with all their might
So remember past is past
After today tomorrow will appear
And then you will find
You will always be on time
Whether or not the clock chimes
For time is clicking
The clock ticking
And the past simply disappearing
To unfold a new day
New way
So close the back door of past memories
Open the door to new possibilities and opportunities
For the new, a glorious reality!

Trains Run in Both Directions

Trains run in both directions
I see you going the other way
Do you see me on the other train
I am not going your way
Best I wish you were going my way
Today I see you again
And I wonder if you notice me
You look but you act like I am here
Or not but I know you see me
Our eyes meet going both ways
But why are we going into different directions
How come you are not on the same trip as me?
I can change trains
Can you change for me?
Tomorrow when I see you
I will be on your side of the platform
Waiting, hoping you are on the same train
As I board the train I look for you
And don't see you
Where are you? I look
I wonder where you are
But you are not there as the doors close
I realize I am on the train
Going in the wrong direction
Disappointed I look out the window
And see you across the platform
Looking earnestly for something
I wonder what it is
And why are you on my platform
And I am on your train
Going in the other direction
I see your eyes catch mine

And you realize I am where
You supposed to be
A smile lets me know
You were looking for me and I for you
And maybe tomorrow we
Will be in the same station
Same time, on the same train
Even though trains run in different directions!

Questionnaire

The questionnaire
I ask
You tell me
What for
Do I call this information?
Save it
Use it
Against you?
For you
Why?
I need this information
I thirst
You drink
I feel
Why?
I need to know you
Now I have it
What I need
You know me
No why not?
No questionnaire?
I ask
You tell me
Never do you ask
What for
Why me
What you need
To do with this info
Because I can't tell you
I need to know
I make money
Selling you

Selling your information
To whom
Whomever I chose
I get paid
For your info
I share you
I am happy
Over and over again
You never asked
What do I do
With your information
I sell
And sell
And sell
You not me
Hope you can see
What has happened
Again and again
I smile
They now know you
From the information
I sold them
About you
Yes you
To whomever
What do you say?
Nothing
Why shocked
Just fill out the application
No I mean the questionnaire
And don't ask any questions!!

You Know Me

You know me
I know you
From where you ask
From where I say
I only know I know you
What do you say
Not from here
I know you in a different way
I remember your face
I know you don't remember me
That is the case
Because your memory
Is not the same as mine
I know we have met many times
That is the way of mankind
We meet we see each other
I go you go another time
We will see each other
The smell the taste the same forever
Only a memory of when we were together
This time we may be apart
But I remember you from the start
Another tune another time
Another chime
When we make music together
Rhythms of old
Rhythms for the Soul
Of you and me
That is how it was then
And way it is to be
But this life is different
But some things remain the same

Love transports game
Love transports time
But not our rhyme
So when we see each other
We don't know when we met
But we definitely know each other
Lovers, sons, daughters, fathers and/or mothers
We had to meet each other
So we can remember
That we are here again
From another life or some other
And we can salute that
We know as we look into
Each other eyes we are familiar.

Stars, Look Listen, Learn

Stars
Sky
Planet
Galaxies
Sound
Light
Air
Water
Don't they speak
Do we listen
Light shines
Do we see
The reflection
Of us
In them
The face reflects
Us
And them
In us
Outside of us
Or so we think
Ancients say
The zodiac feels
Numerologist say numbers talk
Wise Ones say look listen
Hear the whisper
In the wind
Where did the sound come from
How far
How long
We don't know
Is it right or is it wrong

They circle us
Or do we circle them
Or do we all move together
In tandem
To the beat
The sound of the drummer
Beating sounds
Ancient echoes
Chimes sing,
High notes
That shows the stars
Are receiving and sending messages
About life, love
Climbing new heights
As we look up
To see the birds arrive
Then go
As day and night flows
And the stars rest
And wait to display their
Translucence at their best
The chatter is everywhere
If we listen
Nature speaks
Trees remind us of centuries
And we realize
Much we can't explain
Unless we listen, look, learn
And not make any assumption
In vain
All we have to do is look, listen and learn!

Water Come and Go

Water come and go
What else do you know
Nothing that is so
So why you drink tap water, what for
You need to understand
You need to grow
Water is free
You act like you don't see
Water is only two not three
Water is salty
Or water is drinkable
The sea is free
Spring water is for you and me
Why pay for what is given to you free
Is nature now for sale
Can we sell air
Yes they sell oxygen
That comes from air
Even though people complain
They can't get enough
The question is
The answer is breathe
That is all that you need to be
If you sell water
What is next
Organic water is going to be sold
The next dream lie is told
That we need
Until we can create organic air
And have a special fee or tax
Saying that it is rare
So where does water go and come

It goes to the heavens and
Then returns only to be packaged
And sold to you and me
Like air and water we need
But we should not be charged fees
Because it will continue
To come and go
The same as time which ebbs and flow
And this explains why we have to know
It is free!!!

History

History is the best teacher
Who is learning
No one
Or someone
Who knows
Many ignore
Most change
To suit themselves
Like they shop for clothes
Others try to make it fit
Like shoes on a cow
Whose feet are swollen
And too small to comprehend
Why people wear them
History is there for all to see
And read
If they can
But won't help those
Who can't see out of one eye
and blind in the other
Only to see some people
Rewrite what was
 Into what is
Like a new song
Sung in the bathroom
No one can see or hear
Or testify
But you can say it's the gospel
According to who
Only to rubber stamp
Its true meaning
And hide it from

Those who seek the truth
There are those who make it up
In its entirely hoping you would
Believe the hype
And then burn the documents
Like a badly cooked pot of stew
And then pour sauce on it
When we ask a question
Telling us the food has been eaten
And the gravy is only the thing left
So sop it up with a biscuit
Or go away starving
And just remember the taste,
It left in your mouth from memory
Then call it history!

The Quest for Truth

The quest for truth
I seek
I look
I listen
I read
I research
Some more
For many years
Only to find
They lied to me
Why
Is the truth not worthy?
For me to hear
To see
To believe
To know
To expose
Expound
When is it all said and done
The truth
Is what I seek
From you
From her
From them
From all
From they who lie
To you
To me
To all of us
Because they can't believe
Their lying eyes
And they don't want you

To know the truth
Or me
Or us
Anybody
Why?
It might expose them
To us
To the public
As if we don't know
Aren't aware
That they are
All liars
And won't tell the truth
If they knew it
Because they have lied so much
Covered up the truth
Hidden it from us
And themselves
They don't know it themselves
Can't think about it
Can't remember
Don't want to
To painful…
Because so many lies are on top of it
Piled high
Sunk deep
In outer space
They don't know how to search for it
And if they found it
They would be shocked to learn
There is truth out there
Waiting to be discerned
Exposed
Unwrapped
Revealed
To all of us and them
So we would know the truth!

Eons

Eons ago we were given the garden
Now we have the tree and the forest
But fools keep cutting down,
The forest to its knees
In hopes of more greed
The greedy have won
Look at what has been done
Eons ago
We were given all that we needed
From the Earth
At birth
Only to see our people eating meat
And each other
Searching for the perfect burger
Why, to do or die
They keep on trying
To kill all that exists
Telling you it's what they need
Which is a lie
Eons to now
What has transpired
That makes some not understand
It's the mountain top or the mire
Why express what is dire
What our life requires
Wasting what comes natural
To opt for what is manufactured
When you can get
All you need, if you would
Listen to the ancestors
The blue print is there
Unless you can't read then ask where

Do you want to know
Or do you care
Eons we traveled which was normal
No supernatural
Yet we now conduct wars
And spend our tax dollars
Trying to get to the moon
So we can ruin that after…
Why?
How do you know you didn't,
Create the bare moon or mars
Or other places here
And there after
You arrived acting like it is new
And wanting it all for yourself
Like you are due
Another place
To mess up its face
Clear up here first
Then ask, what is a waste
To want or not, what is the haste
Eons it took to get to this place
And now the mirror you can't face
So you pass the blame
On those who don't understand your game
Eons more is the aim
If you stop this foolishness
That is the overriding request
More is better less is best
You can make this a home
Or do what you have been doing
And just be a guest
Who doesn't care about your ancestors
And continue this mess
So eons will turn into less
And we will know you are here
Just as a jest
Before you decide to take a rest
And let eons continue on with the quest!

Sitting on Top of the Mountain

The mountain so big
So high
Why can't you try to climb it
If you could fly
Would you
What is stopping you
This day
Tomorrow
Give it a try
See if you can fly
If you can't walk
Don't just sit and talk
Look up
Not down
Don't be content to just go around and around
The mountain
Go up not down
There is where I can be found
Achieve
Believe
You can do it
Don't let others tell you, you can't
They just deceive you
And tell you to stay down
For another round
Because misery loves company
Pigs like shit
Bums just like to lay and sit
And mud looks good
If you crawl on all fours
But standing and doing opens doors
Start with the first step

Climb until your foot has set
On top of the mountain
Not a spare moment to let
Get away put off tomorrow
What you can accomplish today
Because success is just ahead
When you arrive
You will see
All you didn't believe
That which has been waiting
For you to receive
An unobstructed view of
What you dreamed at the world seat
All is under your feet.

Sacrifice

I sacrificed
I gave in
I let you win
I abdicated
I didn't fight back
I turned the other cheek
I let you hit me
I didn't retaliate
I let you have her
I refused to fight
I laid down my sword
I bit my lip
I clenched my teeth
I squeezed my fist
I let you have her
I did not argue
I waved my rights
I left without her
I sneaked away
I gave you my last dollar
I gave you my last nickel
I gave you my child
I just gave in
I did not follow my career
I let go of my dreams
I did not follow my mind
I did not complete my goals
I did not graduate
I did not finish any tasks
I stopped thinking about it
I sacrificed
So you could do

Be
Realize
Wake up
Open your mind
Open your heart
See clearly
Understand
Learn
Wise up
Stand up
Be broke
Love a reason
Have an epiphany
Drop the excuse
Change your mind
Come to your senses
Choose correctly
Make a decision
Realize
Take an interest
Be totally aware
Make up your mind
And understand I am here for you
And all I want is for you
To try and be the best
You can be
Not for me
But for you
And the children
I sacrificed all for that!

Family

Family
Do you recognize your family
We are family
I make the case
I am from this place
Or am I
I am from that place
Or do I
I am family
You are family
I know it
I realize it
Do you?
Past eons ago
Lifetimes passed
But we are here today
Only memories last
They say
What do they know
Besides dinosaurs
I know you
You know you know me
Even though it was not recently
But as we met
I felt the lifetime's edge away
And then there was only today
And we talked like it was yesterday
But that is how family talk
When we see each other
We all of a sudden remember
That time then and now or was it September
Families linked together

So when you see me
Don't be surprised
I am a part of you
So be advised
That we are similar
I know you look and feel familiar
And we are all together
One another
And family no matter how much time
Has parted, we are still one of a kind
Called family!

Respect Your Elders

Respect your elders
I am older than you
I am older than time
I am older than rhyme
I am your elder
Old as the sun
Old as the moon
I came before the dinosaur
And I came after the insects and more
I lived in the forest
Planted the Garden
For Eden
To make sure all was ready when she came
And she was asked for more just the same
I am older than you
How come you don't respect elders too
You're young and new
Here now thinking this is all you
It is not yours
It is mine
I left for you and your kind
To take care of it for a time
And instead of you making it a bless
You created a mess
Created racism
Like you deserve all this
For yourself talking you're blue blood
No such thing, all who are alive, blood is red
May be blue when you're dead
But you think you're smart
Mensa and all that
Why Einstein showed you, you're not

You think you can tell me what to do
Only thing you tell me is you're a bigger fool
For I am older than you
Trees know more than you
They have done more and seen more
From their view
I have seen mothers come
And children go
Only to come again
To repeat and learn the most important lesson
I am older, wiser, and smarter
And can see for them
I can see if you don't respect the elders
Older than you
You will repeat what I taught you
We elders seen it all
We are available if you call
And will share our wisdom and more
For elders come and go
But our wisdom is here
And all around you and more
So no need to ramble
Tell you are not ample
To handle all these problems
Global warming, health care, greed,
Racism, wars, and more that's raw
Requiring an elder to explain
How to correct this mess
If you don't know ask somebody
Who is an elder or give it a rest
And sure I was here before all this grime
Seen and done all this before
I can also tell you what to do this time
Respect your elders!

Disguises

Disguises
Hiding
Revealing
Not revealing
The truth
Many hide behind
Their masks
In hopes of not being discovered
By those who can see
And those who can't
But seen by people like me
Many hide
Many won't show the real side
Of whom they are
Just take up jobs and professions
That hides who they really are
Their real professions
Giving you the impression
They are this and all that
And think it is ok
As long as they do or go to confession
But disguises can't hide
The ugly they possess
Their true selves are shown
Sooner or later even if they don't confess
The truth of their disguise
Will come to light
Sooner or later, more or less
You can play the game
And assume some fictitious name
Or create some false identity
Even achieve some fame

But who you are and are not
Will remain the same
And tricking those with your
Disguise or mask
Will eventually be revealed
And won't last
For it is like makeup
It is only a disguise
And that is the difference
Between a truth and a lie
Even if you hide behind the
Disguise until the day you die
Being true to yourself
Is the only answer
When are you going to realize
And stop using and abusing
Those who put their trust in you
Only to see now or find out later
The dirt or nonsense you do
To prove you are not real
But just a fantasy
Waiting to be exposed, revealed
And the mask you wear
Is a trick of the eye
For all to see
And make aware
And you are only a disguise
Nothing else you will ever be!

I Don't Know, Do You?

I don't know, do you
Can't say that I will
Can I?
Can you?
Don't know if I could
Don't know if I would
Can't tell
Can't see for looking
Can't want for seeing
Can't be for wanting
I am ok
This way
How are you
Are you to blame
Are you doing the same
As you did yesterday
Or are you trying to do it another way
Tomorrow will it be different
Or will it be the same
Or will the excuse be love
As it was last time you came
I don't know
Do you?
Can you tell
If it was
As it was said
Or is it just an excuse you made
To placate me
As you always do
Or is this just how it is to be
I don't know
Do you?

Who Am I

Who am I
Who are you to ask
Forget who I am
Who are you
Where are you from
Another planet
Here on loan
Why have you come
To do harm
To warn me of those who do
Why don't you look at you
Not me
I can see,
Can you fool who?
Who you fooling
Rest not today
Explain no tomorrow
Claim this is yours?
By a flag
Or is it the gun behind the flag
Why you lie to yourself
You say for self wealth
Why do you need it all
Can't you share some
Greed is your motto
Well I am not you
I can see
Can you?
Can you really see
What you do to me
And us, and them
All because you are blinded
By the wealth of sin
Wake up
See where you've been.

Hear Me?

A whisper
I can hear
Can you hear me
Speak louder
I try but can't
Because my lips are soft
And my voice meek
My words sound weak
But if you listen close
You will see that they are strong
They rhyme like a song
They resonate in your mind
Like a melody
I don't want to shout
But want to make you show
Titillate your mind
Loosen your underpinnings
So you will come closer
Listen carefully
Envision the wonderment
Of my words
My story
All wrapped up in glory
Of how the flow of my poetry
And at night you crawl up closer
To hear me whisper
The sweet something's
That carries in the nights,
Crisp air as the breeze blows down your dress and
Tingles through your strings up to
Shudder your thighs
And make your toes,

Clasp the harp
Between your legs
And cause you to pull the
Cover closer
Thinking of me and no other!

Doors Open

Doors open
Doors close
Doors hoping
It is the right one for you
Doors lead you on the way
Doors lead you astray
Doors help you go away
Choose a door
Choose correct
Don't sit and wait
For someone to lead you their way
Doors lead you correctly toward the ray
Of light
Of might
Or wrong doors lead you to a fight
Or strife
Doors close that is no longer of use
The past is doors that have closed
So new doors can open to the new
Doors meant especially for you
Doors lead you higher
Keep the doors closed that lead you to the mire
So doors are everywhere
Pick the ones that are dear
And help you grow
Or reap what you sow!

No Yesterdays Only Tomorrows

No yesterday's only tomorrows
Rough thinking about it
Wondering why
Gives me a fit
But can't get pass the past
I thought it would last
My mind is made up
I won't forget what I gave up
Who would if it was good
I won't let it go as if I should
I want to remember all of it
As if it happened today
Or just now as if it is it
I know I am worried
But life is like a song
That keeps playing in my head
And I can't turn it off
Like a letter I once read
That said I love what we once had
But it is over and I am so sad
But it is done and I am glad
And I know that you are mad
You can't change the past
And the past is not meant to last
Because there is no yesterdays
Only now, only today
And you must leave what happened then
And be out what is happening now because there are no yesterdays
No one remembers or wants
To live over what happened the other day
But we want and should focus on tomorrow
Only laughs and joy, no sorrows

So lead, know, and tell others
Not to follow
Others who want you to
Look at yesterday
And think you could have been that
Done that, got that
All that but it is gone
You can, though, be that, do that,
Get that, start that, make that
Happen today, not yesterday
For there are no yesterdays
Only tomorrows!

Dust

Why do the collective works collect on your shelf
Why do you not read them
Why does the dust settle
But you don't move it so it is safe
Why do we collect the things
We need to dust
Why does dust remind us
That we don't move
Stationary is the position
Are we so resolute
We can stay in one place
How do we make or show progress
Is it by collecting
Or is it just hoarding and storing
Are people the same to us
Do we collect our dreams
Or do they move along even if we don't
Making progress
Or is the dust of the past
So settled we can't change our minds
We keep trying to dream the same dream
But it has passed on
It has floated by us on the bridge
It has been taken up by the
Last cloud that passed
Surprisingly you seem to be
The only one that doesn't know
There is no dust on the sea
Is that a gentle reminder?
To warm up, change
It's a new day everyday
Or does the rain in the plains

Wash away things that
Went down the drain
And prepares the way
For a fresh new day
Is it possible if we wipe
The dust off
Clear away the clutter of
Our minds
We can breathe better
See further and
Move easier than
Begin to change the behavior
Letting go of the un-useful past
And move to the future at last
We changed views
About me and you
And let Darwin rest
So we can focus on the now
And have the old theories that are jest
And see all as they really are
Humans, people, families
That has the same quest
Live life, enjoy themselves
Prosper and grow to aspire
To do their best
And let others be and take a rest!!

Digging For What

What do the deserts bring up
What is under the sand
Why do man dig so deep
Only to end up still on land
What reveals the sea
Sand reveals only dry land
So what is it that men seek
What is in them that is incomplete
They must dig up all that they see
Kill what is in their way
And say it is what they can do or may
Since they are over other kingdoms
Since they do all for sport and fun
Tombs lie in the sand
Old evidence of historic man
So they can steal their remains
And say they are there not for fame
Yet there is nothing else to really gain
The digging won't lead to China
Digging should be left to the miner
Not to the grave robber
Or those who think there is gold on the moon
Yet can't do anything to help those here
Or even the one's they hold so dear
People walk on the land
Won't dig into their own lives
To help their fellow man
But will try to rip him off
By selling him a swamp or
A house built on sand
And wonder why it falls apart
Then tell you it is not his fault

Stop worrying about the sand
And what's under it
Leave alone the deep blue sea
And stop polluting it
Then blaming it on dirty fish
Which you catch and
Then serve to others on a dish
But concern yourself with what
Is above land
And will help your fellow man!

Dilemma or Do you Think

Is the sky clear
Is the clouds in your mind
Is the sky cloudy
And is your mind clear
Is the time of day now and near
Is the sea far away
Or is the earth turning to meet us
On our way to our destination
Without a fuss
Does the compass
Show us the way
Or are we led by the aroma of the bread
Is food our imagination
Or is life our real dream
And progress a false hope
Do children grow
Or are the children old
Do we reap what we sow
Or can we dream the rainbow
Are we in the dark
Or are we lighting the way
Aiming our boats toward the mark
Is life everywhere
And there is no dead
Or as we sleep,
We are by Grace being led
Do we swim or does
The water meet us and pass the way
Or is life like water than air instead
Can we breathe underwater
And just don't know when asked
What to say

Is the sun touching us
With fingers we think are rays
Or an illusion wakes us up everyday
Does love come to us
Or from us
Or are some of us love and
We live amongst those who hate us
Does the mirror reflect
What we see
Or when we look we see
Who we think is you and me
Does the wind blow
Or is hot and cold expressions
Of the bold
Like babies are warm
And ice is cold
Do rivers move the earth
Or is water too active
To stand still
Or must it continue to drink
Until it get its flow
Questions are answers
Or answers questions
To be known
Does nature wave when we walk by
Or does it hide so we won't
Kill it or make it die
Because we like chemicals and processed foods
Instead of stuff naturally grown
Or does a butterfly flap its wings
Because it is clapping to its success
That it made it thru this mess
And accomplished its quest
I guess I know more or less

Do you know what's best?

The Looking Glass

The looking glass
Can you see
Your reflection
I can see
Have you looked into the mirror
In the present, in the past
Will you look in the future
Can you see
Need glasses
An eye piece
Or do you have 20/20
But blind to what you can see
In front of you, behind, and to the side
Left and right
I am looking
And seeing you
The glass reveals
All I need to see
No door can block my sight
Or your sight
Am I wrong or right
Look at me
See you
Can you be
The picture in the mirror
And can you get into the flow
Life is like a mirror
But there is more to the flow
Can you see it go
Glass reveals what is hidden
Behind the door
With glass unlike the mirror

You can see more
Not some but all
So the mirror looks at you
Glass can see all you do
So look at you
Your present, your future
As we pass through time
Yes I can see you mime
Your way through
But you must clean and clear
The glass
And look beyond their masks
And do what is required
For all you want, need
Or you ask
But remember I can see you
Through the looking glass!

Where Does the Music We Hear Come From

Does the music we hear now
Come from then
Or is it from now
Is it being repeated
From eons ago

And is it saved and its vibrations
Are only echoes
From the past
That we hear in the present
And will hear in the future
Does it change
Or do our minds change
Does the key notes ring in our ear
And we play from memories
And listen with a familiar ear
Does the sound vibrations,
Trigger our own inner harps
And we repeat what we hear
Are we ancient beings
Only echoes of our real self
Or are we sentient beings
New to an old environment
Old songs played a new way
Or are we tuning in
On a radio wave
Or are attuned to the musical melody
Of original notes being
Tapped into and played
For our benefit to remind

Us who we are
Or the never-ending soul vibrations
Of realms where music
Is another language
To communicate on
Soulful levels the way
Higher level masters interpret the
Cosmos of their mind
Knowing they have not
Reached the end of their songs
Or is the music like steps
Moving us along a never ending saga
So we keep playing our melody
To become part of the infinite harmony
That entices us to our
Own greatness
That some miss or mistake only for their sake
When it belongs to all
Of us the human race_
We all are musicians,
Players, singers, in a universal symphony!

Is Talk Cheap

Is talk cheap
Is talk expensive
How much does it cost us
When we talk
Can it be measured
Who sets the scale
What is gained
How much is profit
What is loss
Can it be traded
How much are those promises worth
Hard to measure?
Why, can't see it
Not looking
Can't hear
Don't want to
Think talk is cheap
Is what goes in the mouth
More expensive than
What comes out the mouth
Who's to measure
How long tall or short
Can I measure it
With my yard stick
Or can it reach the sound barrier
Does it cause ringing
In the ears
Because what I said is so heavy
So profound
Or is it?
Or do you think it is cheap
I say, depends on who's talking

Whether they are short talk
Long, skinny or fat
Is where it's at
Speak your word
Say what you got to say
Don't save it for another day
Talk isn't cheap
It is only the talker
That measures his talk
His word
Lame or great
Profound or a noun
So say worthy things
So your words won't be considered cheap!

Sound Theories

Sound theories
A sound makes a noise
A yell is loud
A whisper is hardly heard
Noise comes from the hoofs of the herd
Does a tree make a noise when it falls
Do broken promises make noise
If I scream can you hear why
Does the echo in space arrive on Earth
If I whisper will you listen
If I holler will you shut up
And not listen
Does the small voice
Ripple across the plains
Can I vibrate your mind
Can I make you holler
If I whisper
Can you talk without moving your lips
And can I still hear you?
Does the sound barrier reverberate noise
Are notes singing on a page
Can you hear the melody playing in my ear
Is there silence in your mind
The sound you make when you are asleep
Is to make me know you are awake
Or alive
Is there music blowing through the trees
Chasing the wind to silence
When you try to cry
Or is all of this just sound theory?

Language

Language the way of communications
From ancient times to now
Language
Way of speaking and writing
Who's who talking
From the beginning till now
Language
The way
The flow
The barrier
The breakthrough
Who created the first
Why we talk
Just to open our mouth
Or do we have something to say
False or real
What is the big deal
Why don't we use telepathy
Now telephony
Or do we again go to language
The way of words
The meaning of the word
What we say
What are we going to do
Even if we don't
Do we know
Do we say
How do we know how to communicate
Earlier then now, late
One language in the beginning
No, many languages with the same meaning
All used to communicate

Even if we say nothing
We talk
Laugh
Sing
Holler
Why bother
We want to communicate
That is the language
But so many
How do we communicate of late
We learn your way
We learn how to say
What we wish to convey
In someone else's language
Now many talking
Using language to communicate
You learn mine
I learn yours
This way we learn many kinds
Of languages
Languages and cultures
From the beginning, now into the future
So we can all say
I'm talking your language
You understanding mine
It is time we all have
One common language
To communicate then
We all can say you are talking my
Language
Out loud
Or silently
There is one language
It is love!

Poor is the Crime

Poor is the crime
Waste not, want not its time
People suffer everywhere
Their principles they hold so dear
They love and they fear
Each other
For another
Who take from the poor
To make themselves rich
While others sip water from a ditch
And quench their thirst
While those who have
Too much say they are first
First to commit
Last to pay
But first to collect
And first to redirect
Funds from those in need
To their accounts
With a plea
They need more....
To show their worth
What we don't know, what for
They can't spend
But that is not the plan
It's just to show
Like the championship dog
Holding a pose
So the poor can look up
To them when they pass with a cup
Saying I am poor
And honest, what for

Because I already committed a crime
And it's time
I pay for it
So everyone can see I did it
I begged and swore
I will not act like those
Who steal, cheat, and forged
Just to show that they are
Innocent of being poor!

America's Learning Disability

Have you not learned?
Do you ever learn?
Do you remember Lemuria?
Do you remember Atlantis?
Do you not see Great Britain?
Can't you see clearly and yearn
For a new way
Life is not about a cloudy day
The past is the past
But also a tool of what happened last
Last is history
Past is a memory
Don't just think about victories
But learn from all that has been
All that has been done
To teach you about another way
Messages that the past history tries to convey
That you are not learning the right way
To be like great Britain
Who came to power
Robbing, stealing, warring like barbarians
Then coming to America to do the same
Only worse
By wanton killing, slavery, wars and worse
Under the guise that this is a democracy
Or is it a lie and this is just a idiosyncrasy
A lack of vision
Multitudes of unwise decisions
Money can't buy love or happiness
And you have proven intelligence,
Doesn't lead to wisdom
If experience is our best teacher

You have failed the course
And doomed to repeat, there is no other recourse
Only way to win
Stop this nonsense and all the sin
And try to change the course
So you can win
The best way to win hearts and minds
Not by media tricks of the trade
But by trying to live and make the grade
That is put upon those who understand
And have learned that pills won't help this
But cut it out like you do a cist
And practice what you preach
And correct Americas' learning disability
So that real peace, love and happiness
Can be in this lifetime within reach!

A Monkey Said

A monkey said
Monkey see monkey do
I ponder the thought
I ponder the thing
I ponder the reality
In disbelief
How could it be
When did it happen
I was told it could not
Why was I ill informed
I ponder that
And wonder
Who fooled me
Who tricked me
I am in disbelief
So I ponder the thought
So I ponder the idea of it
Who would do this
Try to play tricks on me
How dare you
I know better
Don't you?
I see through your scheme
Sure blame it on me
I am sorry
I won't accept
Nor will I let
You blame me without regret
That I caused all of this
Surely you jest
Ha, you come from me
Ha, give it a rest

Nature sees through your play
And my ancestors won't employ
That story
That human came from mankind
Not after the mess you've created
When we let you into our home
As a quest
Only to find out you
Don't respect us
And blame is on evolution
That causes for your endless revolution.

What Are You Waiting For

Stars wake up and are alive
The sun comes out to play
The moon dances in the sunlight
To light up the night
The sea is moving and transversing the earth
The sky collects the dew
And raises up to let you see
It anew
What are you waiting for
The flowers open up and play a tune
Are you listening, do you hear
The chirps of the birds
Singing the melody
The animals stomping in the background
The wind blowing vibes
Planets spinning in sequence
To spin the wheel of life
You supposed to know
It's all for you
What are you waiting for
Get yourself attuned
Spring forth anew
Climb to a higher place
So you can see
And adjust your view
What are you waiting for
Can't you see
It is now for you
Wait no longer
Don't wait for the many
Because there is only a few
That will wake up after you
But then many once they see you
Wake up now
Sleep no longer
Your time is due!

Open the Door

Open the door
Open the door to new possibilities
To new ways
To open the door to new heights
Open the door
Of your mind
To your heart
Open, open to the new you
Close the old doors
That leads to the past
Close the old doors
That were past relationships
Close the old doors
To failure and disappointments
And realize they are all gone
For good
Never to return
So let go of the knob
Turn now to the new
Pick up the new keys
Grab hold of the knob
And open the new door
To success
Open the new door to a better life
Open the new door to no strife
Open the new door to a happy life
Let in the sunshine
Open the door
Step in out of the darkness
Step in out of the shade
Step in out of the viewing stands
Bask in the sun light

As the rays caress your face
Feel the new ground under your feet
And hear the aroma
Titillate your senses
As it beckons you on
Step fully through the new door
Step fully into the new
Step fully into the new you
You have been waiting for
And know it is here
What you were waiting,
Hoping, wishing, for
And know it is waiting for you
Naked, fully exposed, open
Unabridged, no explanation
Now just you, just new
You have arrived and it is time
Breathe deep a sigh of relief
And know that the door has opened
You have stepped in and
Are now new renewed
And you have truly won
A new life!

The Phoenix Rises

The phoenix rises
The dragon shakes his tail
They try to give you the nod
Which way to go
Down is not up
Up is down
What is the problem
What causes you to be confounded
About all that is round
I rise, I move
I have being
What do you intend to do
Why does the phoenix fly
Why does the dragon have a tail
Why do you walk to where you have to go
Which way is up
How come you don't know
You have been time and time again shown
You have a heart
So does the phoenix
And the dragon who is old
Don't you get it
Why are you so cold
Why can't you fly
Because you don't know which way to go
Shake off the seeds of hate
Get rid of the envy and jealousy
That you think glitters like gold
Relieve yourself of the stuff,
You carry
That burdens the soul
Take flight

To be whom you have known
To be or not to be
Is the dilemma
Not the question
How you cannot see
Is the question
What you need to do to become free
That is the answer
Between you and me
The ashes are gone
The phoenix has flown
The dragon awaits
For you to give up your ignorance
And requires you to come home
So you can learn to just be!

Always Becoming

I am the butterfly
Fresh from the cocoon
I am the baby
Just born today
I am the river
Beginning to surge forth
I am the volcano
Stretching my arms
Pushing my lava to the surface
I am the poet
Beginning to express myself
I am the bird preparing
For a new song
As I take flight on.......
On a new path
New journey
Like the student
First day in college
The African American
Just left home
And now must make it on his own
I am seeing endless possibilities

The sky is the limit
As I look through the glass ceiling
I am at the brink
Of successful thinking
Wondering why on revolution
On waste and haste
On the pace of my rise
On the evolution of my being
I see all the doors opening

The ones that lead me to the top
To new heights
Only to see the new mountain
The next climb

My sneakers are put on
And laced
For the run before the start of the game
I am poised for the fame
That I see
And can reach
That is fair game
I run with the Cheaters
To reach my goals
First without reservations
Or misgivings
I throw caution to the wind
I reach and grab the golden ring
And hope all that glitters
I now hold in my
Hand is really gold
As I prepare my next role
To be king and find my queen
And then reign in the
Kingdom of my dreams
On to the next great thing

Yes I am always moving
Leading the rainbow
Following the stars
As new galaxies appear
To show they are in tune
With my growth
And are beckoning me on to greater heights
Intergalactic expectations
And to boldly go where no one else
Has dared to be or go
To fulfill their dreams
I am becoming who I am

I am growing to be who I am to be
I am and will always be climbing
Even if they have to build
A ladder to get there
Because I have just begun
And I will never be done!

Pushing People

Pushing people to change their ways
Pushing people to get out of your way
Pushing people to take up your way
Pushing those aside who don't abide
Pushing those who are moving at their own stride
Pushing those on the straight and narrow
To make way for those
Who are crook-it and wide
Saying it is the only way to increase their stride
Pushing ever pushing saying they are right and everyone not traveling…
At their speed is not quite in their sight
Ever pushing going their way
Saying to all, "you can do today"
Not realizing that it is not here to stay
Steal their artifacts you say
The culture is in the people
Not in the jewelry or the clay
But you don't know you just push your way
See cultures as only a temporary delay
Of getting what you want
And things and people in your way
Tall buildings does not a park make
Nature is not in the city
But in the park and the lake
Concrete jungles are only fake
And all that industrial revolution is not that safe
So keep pushing just for pushing sake
Killing everything in your path
Is one of the reasons for natures' wrath
And it will take your changes
And push them aside
To let you know that you still have to obey

People and culture and their timeless strides
That keeps them ever moving forward and onward
That keeps them striving for longevity
Without pushing anyone aside
So pushing may work for you
And what you are trying to do
But you will not push all to be like you
The world will turn at the same speed
And cultures will teach you about nature
And how things fall in place
Without creating a lot of waste
Not only here but in outer space!!!

Light Travels Together

Do we travel together
Do we travel along a stream together
Do we ride the waves of time
Do we turn the millennium clock together
Are we watching the same play
Are we viewing the same program
Are we on the same wavelength
Or are we attuned to each other's frequency
Can it be we traveled the galaxies together
Soared to new heights
Or did I leave you behind
Did you refuse to climb with me
To the highest mountain
Were you lured away to another place
Or are you moving full circle
Toward me or away from us
I remember you on the way
We were supposed to arrive at the same place
At the same time
But I came, I looked, I saw
All but you
Where are you now?
Where are all the others
Are we all on the way on the trail
Meeting at the top
Did we pass each other without a wave
But just a sigh
I think we are traveling
I will put out the call
For us to arrive without delay
To a place only a light away
And it will be a glorious day
And it will prove that the
Light has led us to the same way.

Power

Power is awaken
Power is taken
Power is shaken
But won't go to sleep
Power is alive
Power does not wait
Power overtakes
Power doesn't risk
Power exists
Power controls
Power is neither young nor old
Power is used to move mountains
And hurricanes
So is power from wind and rain
Power adapts
Power corrupts
Power knows its own way
Power knows what to say
As it expresses itself
Each and every day
Power succeeds
Where weakness fails
Power grows
Like the power generated from the fin of a whale
Power generates
As it inundates
Above and below
Just as it reaps, it sows
Use the power
Just like a women..
Uses the flower
Power unleashed

Can harm
Power can heal
Or change chaos to calm
How do you use your power?
To heal, to harm
Or do you use your power
To transform the organic farm
And show others
You are a lover?

Conundrum

Mind	found
Body	made
Soul	copy
Spirit	original
Light	mix it up
Life	face
Wrong	back
Right	in
Up	out
Down	what
Left	how
To the right	why
Bottom	I said who
On top	whom
Where are you	ha
Speak	laugh
Shut up	cry
Open	sign
Close	done
No	nope
Yes	brain
I said yes	feet
Bless	arms length
East	close to me
West	what did you say
North	something
South	nothing
Right on	I bet
Onward	you lose
Run	I win
Walk	give
Path	receive
Last	question
The answers	the conundrum!

Ancient Echoes

Ancient echoes
Left right
Way to go
Now can do
All asked
Because
You are ancient
Love the old
Heart is whole
Ancient echoes
Ring below
And above
The echo
Of your song
Mind singing
All on hold
Now many
Now unfold
So you can see
Ancients
Around you
Want you to be
Immortal!